THE ROYAL SOCIETY OF
PORTRAIT PAINTERS
CENTENARY EXHIBITION 1991

Her Majesty The Queen, Captain General Royal Regiment of Artillery 1975 by David Poole (President)
Lent by The Officers of The Royal Regiment of Artillery

THE ROYAL SOCIETY OF PORTRAIT PAINTERS

PATRON
HER MAJESTY THE QUEEN

CENTENARY EXHIBITION 1991
4th May to 31st May

THE MALL GALLERIES
The Mall, London SW1

ACKNOWLEDGEMENTS

The Council and members of the Royal Society of Portrait Painters wish to pay tribute to those who have lent pictures from both private and public collections for this exhibition.

The Society would further like to thank the following, for the help and generosity in making this exhibition possible:

James Bourlet & Sons Limited

The Carroll Foundation

Clerical Medical Investment Group

Coutts and Co.
(for further assistance during the Centenary year)

Michael Darby

Mrs. Cowan Dobson

Federation of British Artists

The Master of the Worshipful Company of Glaziers

Graig Shipping plc

Guinness plc

C. Hoare & Co.

Inchcape plc

Mr and Mrs G.F. Jacobs

The Kirby Laing Foundation

Roger Lark & Sedgwick

The Viscount Leverhulme

Lloyds Bank plc

Christopher Lloyd

Marks & Spencer
(for their generous contribution without which the publication of this catalogue would not have been possible)

John Mowlem & Co.

Charles Noble

The Royal Bank of Scotland

Royal Society of British Artists

Unilever

THE
CARROLL FOUNDATION
AWARD

The Society wishes to acknowledge the considerable interest
shown by the Carroll Foundation in encouraging young artists and furthering
the aims of the Royal Society of Portrait Painters.

A Silver medal together with a cheque for £3,000 is awarded annually
to the successful artist under the age of 35.

In addition the Society gratefully acknowledges the generous contribution
by the Carroll Foundation towards the expenses incurred in the mounting of
this Centenary Exhibition.

Fig.1 James McNeill Whistler
Harmony in Grey and Green: Miss Cicely Alexander
Tate Gallery, London

THE EARLY YEARS OF
THE ROYAL SOCIETY OF PORTRAIT PAINTERS

by Kenneth McConkey

I've just finished a portrait – a millionaire's wife, Lady Rockett .... Of course it was my 'Slummer' that got me the job. Women have been raving about that girl's head; and it isn't bad, though I say it. I had to take a studio at a couple of day's notice – couldn't ask Lady Rockett to come and sit at that place of mine in Battersea; a shabby hole. She isn't really anything out of the way as a pretty woman; but I've made her – well you'll see it at some exhibition this winter, if you care to. Pleased? Isn't she pleased! And her husband, the podgy old millionaire baronet, used to come every day and stare in delight. [1]

These deeply cynical words come from the mouth of Norbert Franks, the fictional painter in George Gissing's novel, *Will Warburton*. Franks, we are told, had achieved success at the Royal Academy exhibition with a picture of a pretty waif from the slums which, although it was shown under the title, *The Ministering Angel,* was habitually referred to in conversation as *The Slummer.* In a quite calculated way the painter hoped to ensnare rich clients with a sentimental image which would reveal his talents. Once caught in the studio-trap, their true features might act as the incidental stimulus to a naked act of ego-inflation, gratifying both sitter and patron. The final accolade for this confection was to be seen "... at some exhibition ..."

Franks is, of course, a caricature and his motives were not generally shared by the portraitist of the turn of the century. It was nevertheless the case that the growing market tended to pull many painters away from classical, Biblical or contemporary scenes into the less speculative domain of portraiture.

The burgeoning of art societies and entrepreneurial exhibitions in the late nineteenth century created new possibilities for specialization amongst painters. This in turn reflected expanding markets. There were societies of pastellists and painter-etchers alongside 'reformed' and 'unreformed' watercolour societies. There were 'black and white' exhibitions as well as mixed shows of 'fair children'

and 'fair women'. Oil painters' societies flourished and the competition led to a re-ordering of priorities in some older establishments. Whistler as President of the Society of British Artists, applied radical policies, although his acumen in obtaining the royal patronage was insufficient to protect him from the Society's conservative core. Youthful avant-garde debate coupled with dissatisfaction with the Royal Academy determined the early years of the New English Art Club. For all its seeming heterogeneity, the Academy was too exclusive. Its doors were closed to whole sections of the artistic production of its day and in certain genres its exhibitions could no longer be considered representative. In this respect the growing popularity of portraiture presented a problem.

In the High Victorian period, British portraiture was a lost art. The prominence in London of international court painters like Franz Xavier Winterhalter served to underline the lack of demand. Victorian worthies preferred not to flaunt their wealth and personal prestige in portraits. Only by the 1870s did these attitudes begin to change. The growth of literacy and illustrated journalism created new needs which reverberated through public exhibitions. There were, by the 1880s, different ways of dealing with fame. The craft of making a likeness was rethought; the dull verisimilitude of Academy portraits was rejected. It was because the Royal Academy had little room for portraits other than those of academicians, that younger portrait-painters banded together in the spring of 1891. *The Magazine of Art* reported the first meeting of sixteen painters, "the front rank of Outsiders" in Archibald John Stuart Wortley's studio at 68 Westbourne Terrace. It was recognized that, "... the present uncertainty attending the acceptance of portraits, however well painted, by all but Academicians is at the root of the new movement." [2] A committee chaired by Wortley and comprising James Jebusa Shannon, Percy Jacomb Hood, Arthur Melville and the Hon. John Collier was formed to set up an exhibition. At the second general meeting in April, Shannon's proposal for the formation of a Society of Portrait Painters was carried. Wortley was its first President. [3]

9

The "movement", whilst it had this compelling *raison d'etre,* had broader aims based upon a recognition of the increased popularity of portraiture. By the 1890s the portrait had aesthetic as well as commercial interest. The recognized path from controversial narrative pictures to the lucrative safety of portraiture was not so simple as it is made to appear in Gissing's account. A bewildering range of choices implying different kinds of social caché, faced the client shopping for a likeness, as much as the young painter, building a reputation. To some extent the Society of Portrait Painters tried to demonstrate this range in their first exhibition. Aside from showing recent examples of their own work, the members gathered revered portraits by accepted masters and invited prominent foreign artists to send examples of their work. The strategy, in the opinion of a number of reviewers worked admirably to establish the group "in the foremost rank of art societies of the day."[4] Elsewhere, the savage *Athenaeum* critic was prepared to dismiss the members in favour of the masters. The show was "... not important still less attractive ... with about twenty exceptions of high merit."[5] These were listed as the works of the older Academicians such as Sir John Millais, G.F. Watts and Sir Frederic Leighton. James McNeill Whistler, exhibiting *Arrangement in Grey and Black, no.1: the Artist's Mother* and *Harmony in Grey and Green: Miss Cicely Alexander* (fig.1) was faintly praised. The tension that this contrast implied – *The Artist's Mother* had only been shown at the Royal Academy after considerable argument – was made the subject of a didactic essay by the novelist George Moore. Dismissing the ancient Academicians, Moore praised the Japanese effects of *Cicely Alexander.* Its painter had combined "fragments of his choice into an exquisite whole," while in Sir John Millais' art there was "no selection; the model is copied – and only sometimes with sufficient technical skill."[6] Thus the first of the Society's exhibitions brought to the forefront of the art world the relationship between the likeness and the work of art – the former tainted with commercialism, the latter shrouded in mystery.

The distinguished foreign artists, and the 'talented' lady portraitists whose work was on display did not provide reconciliation to the opposing camps of contemporary painters.[7] The President of the Society was a follower of Millais and even shared his passion for field sports.[8] J.J. Shannon, on the other hand had been associated with the New English Art Club and

Fig.2 Walter Richard Sickert *George Moore*
Tate Gallery, London

was more related to the Sargent strand of portrait painting.[9] This *premier coup* type of painting was notable in the ranks of the French contingent, which included a picture by Sargent's teacher, Carolus Duran, as well as a work by the heir to his Paris studio, Giovanni Boldini. We can only surmise at the response to Fantin Latour's *Un atelier aux Batignolles,* the important group portrait of Manet and members of the Impressionist circle, which had been completed in 1870.

Despite the fact that the first exhibition incurred a loss of £192.10.7 the members were keen to proceed with planning the next exhibition. Critics were equally keen to see if the high standards of the first show could be sustained. The consensus was that, if anything, the 1892 exhibition had surpassed its predecessor. Modern masterpieces included Millais' *Mrs. Bischoffsheim,* Orchardson's *Master Baby* and Leighton's *Sir Richard Burton,* augmented by Ouless's *Cardinal Manning,* and Boldini's pastel portrait of *Guiseppi Verdi,* both of which had been featured in the Paris Exposition Universelle of 1889. Alma Tadema, Watts and Whistler were among those brought into membership in 1892. The exhibition was also notable for the inclusion of Glasgow School portraitists, John Lavery and James Guthrie. Lavery's *Portrait Studies* "had that graciousness and distinction which are rarely lacking in his performances," while Guthrie's full-length of *Miss Spencer* was regarded as "lacking his usual force."[10]

George Moore (fig.2) once again used the exhibition to advance the contemporary debate about modern painting. Many younger painters were tackling full-length portraits. The seeds of second generation French realism, inspired by Velazquez and Goya, and promoted by Whistler and Sargent, had taken root in Britain in the generation of Lavery, Shannon, Guthrie, Loudan, Jack, Da Costa and many others.[11] Its principal form was the full-length portrait executed upon a perpendicular double square-shaped canvas, seven feet by three feet six inches. It was this phenomenon which drew Moore's attention. "Speaking broadly", he declared, "... the life-size portrait may be said to be the test by which the painter is ultimately judged. In all other forms of art, evasion, subterfuge, deception, is possible, but in the life-size portrait shortcomings at once become failings. The painter shows all he knows and all he doesn't know, he reveals himself to us as he is, and we know him as we never knew him before."[12] In such claims portrait painting regained its position in the hierarchy of artistic value. Landscape, genre and grand manner history painting offered less of a challenge. And this particular mode, the figure presented in its entirety as first developed by Titian and perfected by Velazquez, was the ultimate test. Already the mythology of Whistler's perfectionism, the endless sittings, the wrecking and revising, the nervous strain of performance, to which Sickert referred in his celebrated critique of Whistler's method, was beginning to take hold.[13] Some young artists were too sensitive and too subservient to the vogue. James Guthrie's *Miss Spencer*, for instance, was no more than "a Whistlerian arrangement of tints" in Moore's eyes.[14]

With the serious critical attention accorded to the second exhibition, the Society was firmly established in the art calendar. Its finances were still relatively shaky, and the managing committee realized that the only way to financial security was through producing exhibitions of high quality in prestigious venues. In March 1893 they were proud to announce to members that they had secured the "new and beautiful" Grafton Galleries for the forthcoming exhibition in May.[15] This central venue, designed by the architects, Wimperis and Arber, in Grafton Street, New Bond Street,

contained four large galleries, "with every arrangement careful forethought could supply to ... the comfort of visitors."[16] There was a make-or-break tone in the letter of exhortation to members to send in their best work as "this year will prove whether the Portrait Society deserves or does not deserve to become a permanent and valuable institution." The organizers had noted that some members preferred to send their best work to long established exhibitions and risk rejection, rather than devote themselves exclusively to the Society. In the event the young lions, Lavery and Guthrie returned and they were augmented by Sargent – now being recognized as the most formidable of the new portrait painters.

The Society enlisted Sargent's support at an opportune moment. In 1893 the painter had displayed two major portraits, those of *Lady Agnew of Lochnaw* (fig.3) and *Mrs Hugh Hammersley* at the Royal Academy and the New Gallery respectively.[17] In the case of *Lady Agnew,* the whispers in the press that this was a modern masterpiece, conferred instant celebrity upon the sitter. Sargent was no longer risky to potential clients. From 1893 onwards he was launched upon a long sequence of glittering images which played up the supreme self-confidence of his

Fig.3 John Singer Sargent *Lady Agnew of Lochnaw*
National Galleries of Scotland, Edinburgh

Fig.4 Jacques-Emile Blanche *Aubrey Beardsley*
National Portrait Gallery, London

subjects. Phlegmatic and at times embarrassingly inarticulate, he soothed himself for the tyranny of a diary full of commissions, by fingering snatches of Fauré on the piano. By 1908, when it was beginning to seem to critics that his brush was becoming "quite rhetorical", he gave up portrait painting and would thereafter only answer requests with swift charcoal drawings.[18] So successful in turn were these that the Society staged a small retrospective of them within its exhibition of 1916.[19]

More than any artist of his generation, Sargent signified the complete assurance of the *premier coup* method. He could, as one contemporary remarked, drop an eye into its socket like dropping a poached egg on to a plate. His work caught the imagination of the public to such an extent that Sickert was compelled to invent the term 'Sargentolatry'.[20] It has been argued that his portraits contain a mysterious distillation of the opulence of the age and it must be the case that Solomon, Bacon, Jack, Da Costa and others depended upon his virtuosity to give authority to theirs. The painter therefore stood for a phenomenon greater than himself and it was this which helped to create the conditions for the acceptance of a much wider range of portrait painting than had been possible in the mid-century.

This growing fascination with portraiture, upon which the Society capitalized did not, alas, pave the way to financial stability. As an artists' self-help organization, its meetings were orderly and it functioned with the minimum of bureaucracy. The lack of firm control of its affairs precipitated a crisis in October 1896 when Stuart Wortley called for the accounts. A state of great confusion was revealed. The chairman called for the secretary to attend a special meeting, but he could not be found, nor could the Society's chequebook. An accountant was called in and after two weeks of close scrutiny, a deficiency of £319.0.6 was revealed. A partial solution was found by extracting a levy of £5 from all members.[21]

These regrettable affairs had no effect upon the quality of the Society's exhibitions. In 1895, for instance, the French contingent was headed by exceptional works from Gustave Courtois and Dagnan Bouveret. Jacques-Emile Blanche showed portraits of *George Moore* and *Aubrey Beardsley*. (fig.4) This latter work was regarded as a "somewhat cruel caricature." "The pictorial freaks of this clever artist," wrote one disgruntled reviewer, "do not enhance his reputation as a man of taste."[22] Yet it was precisely as a man of taste that Blanche was respected by his English artist colleagues. Undeterred the painter submitted *Fritz Thaulow and his Family* the following year, and although "less finished than English portraits usually are," the work was grudgingly approved.[23]

From the start the most risky foreign exhibitor was the Italian painter, Giovanni Boldini. There had been almost a sigh of relief on the part of *The Magazine of Art* when this artist, "so wilful and cynical in his vulgarity" had contributed an uncontroversial child portrait in 1892.[24] Boldini was so renowned for the *décolletage* of his female sitters that Sickert dubbed him the "*non pareil* parent of the wriggle and chiffon school."[25] His rendering of *Lady Colin Campbell* (fig.5) entirely typifies this type of portrait. Yet it was a male portrait in 1903 which was "amazing in its unscrupulous vulgarity."[26] The highlights were so extremely accentuated that the whole figure seemed as though polished like patent leather. Only the Spanish painter, Ignacio Zuloaga, could compete in greenish phosphorescent highlights which imparted "some diabolical radiance" upon his sitters.

These extremes marked the borders of the Portrait Painters' exhibitions. The other end of the spectrum

Fig.5 Giovanni Boldini *Lady Colin Campbell*
National Portrait Gallery, London

Fig.6 John Lavery *Miss Mary Burrell*
The Burrell Collection, Glasgow

for his fashion plate superficiality. As early as 1891 his commercial success was noted by *The Art Journal*.[29]

It grew as the studio roster of "white satin duchesses" lengthened.[30] For some critics it was through Shannon that modern portrait painting could be seen as "one of the most profound sources of artistic inspiration."[31] Shannon's prominence in the Royal Academy and the New Gallery in the Edwardian years made him the logical choice to become the third President of the Society of Portrait Painters, after the death of William Quiller Orchardson in 1910.[32] He was the first of the new generation of portraitists of the 1880s, the original proposer of the Society, to assume its highest office.

Within a short time of becoming President, Shannon was presented with a proposition by the Fine Art Committee of the Coronation Exhibition at Shepherds Bush, that the Society should show a retrospective selection of the work of members.[33] A Dinner was held on the Society's behalf on 19 July 1911, with J. Lyons and Co. Ltd. providing a menu at five shillings a head. On this occasion Shannon rose to announce that,

> *His Majesty the King had been graciously pleased to command that the Society which has now attained its 21st year, shall be known in future as "the Royal Society of Portrait Painters".[34]*

By 1911 the character of the Society's exhibitions had changed rapidly. Younger painters like Rothenstein, Strang, Orpen and Nicholson had joined. There was often a desire among these artists to break the conventions of portraiture, taking in the setting as well as the sitter. Personality could be expressed through the arrangement of a drawing room. Discussing one notable portrait-interior by Orpen, *The Studio* critic commented, "instead of competing with the sitter, accessories can be made to assist the expression of his personality, reflecting his tastes and the world in which he moves."[35] Pictures of this type, on a cabinet scale, recalling seventeenth century Dutch interiors, were produced before and after the Great War and with some artists and sitters, they supplanted the perpendicular seven foot canvas. They often incorporated a new Ingrist precision – best seen in the work of Brockhurst, Gunn and Jagger – painters of the teens, twenties and thirties who reasserted the iconic quality of the portrait.

These trends, were reflected largely in the paintings of New English Art Club imports into the Portrait

was defined by the venerable Victorians. "The mere fact that Mr. Watts contributes some of the work of his prime, raises the exhibition above the ordinary level of contemporary shows," wrote *The Athenaeum* in 1902.[27] Even conservative critics could not ignore the central position of painters like Shannon, Lavery, Guthrie, Solomon, Furse and Jacomb Hood. Sometimes attacked for being trite and formulaic in their performances – as when Lavery showed *Miss Mary Burrell* (fig.6) in 1895 – they, nevertheless formed the central caucus of the Portrait Painters.[28] Of the group, J.J. Shannon was most frequently assailed

Painters. Competition among the art societies for public attention continued into the early years of the century. Portraits occupied a prominent place in New English exhibitions as they now did at the Royal Academy, the New Gallery and the International Society of Sculptors, Painters and Gravers. The International Society hosted "Fair Women" exhibitions, specifically devoted to female portraits among which the dominant aesthetic, seen in the work of Jack, Mann, De Glehn and Da Costa, was an eighteenth century one.[36] A potentially serious challenge to the central position occupied by the Society came, however, in 1907 with the founding of the Modern Society of Portrait Painters. Although it boasted the likes of Kelly, J.D. Fergusson and Philpot, the quality of Modern Society shows was not always high.[37] Its first exhibition was something of a damp squib, lacking, in the opinion of one reviewer, "grandeur and the element of surprise."[38] This impression was confirmed by others when in later years the Modern Portrait Painters showed at the Fine Art Society.[39]

Competition arguably consolidated the Royal Society's position. Its shows had struck a happy medium between the conventional and the avant-garde. Soirées and banquets now became part of the annual round, although the outbreak of War put an end to such affairs. Various attempts were made at fund-raising during the War and a special 'R.P.' exhibition was staged at the Walker Art Gallery, Liverpool in 1917. The Society was slow to resume its activities after the War and in 1920 it was made temporarily homeless by the expiry of its Grafton Gallery lease, taken out in 1912. It borrowed the Royal Academy for the exhibition of 1921, showed at the R.B.A. galleries in 1923 and was back in the Academy in 1924, 1925 and 1926. There was no exhibition in 1927 but a short term lease on the Grafton restored continuity for the next three years. Thereafter the Portrait Painters secured a permanent home at the Institute Galleries, until they were bombed in 1940.

In 1923 the 'beloved' Shannon died and was replaced by Sir William Orpen, a President remembered for his magnanimity in instantly writing a cheque to settle the Society's debts.[40] Orpen was replaced by Lavery in 1931 and he, in turn, presided over the Society's affairs until his death in 1941.

Changes in portraiture reflected changes of attitude and orientation in Britain between the Wars. The Society's exhibition of 1917, for instance, was criticised for containing "too many portraits of the smooth photographic type."[41] It was in danger, once again, of being marginalized, or of appearing old fashioned. New perspectives were graphically expressed by Charles Marriott in 1923 when he noted how well Sargent's Wertheimer suite, painted around the turn of the century, fitted into the National Gallery. "Mr. Sargent rounds off the period in which painting may be said to have ministered to 'the pride of the eye'..." he declared.[42] "For better or worse we have lost faith in appearances." A few years later, James Laver took up this crisis and change in contemporary portraiture. For the young woman of the twenties Sargent might show that she had "drunk champagne the night before and had a headache.." Lavery would flatter her *modiste* rather than her, and Orpen would show her merely as a "highlight amid (her) own bric-a-brac."[43]

The painter of modern young women like Lady Diana Manners and Miss Elizabeth Johnson (fig.7) was indisputably Ambrose McEvoy. His sitters were often caught in the act of taking off. Their diaphanous layers of gauze and silk float free from the bondage of brooches, pins, jewellry and excessive coiffure. They are about to leave the studio for a more exciting world. Evan Charteris wrote to Mrs McEvoy that her

Fig.7 Ambrose McEvoy *Miss Elizabeth Johnson*
Glasgow Art Gallery and Museum

Fig.8 James Jebusa Shannon *Flora*
Glasgow Art Gallery and Museum

husband's work was "like coming from a dark forest into a summer clearing."[44] Older artists, Shannon, for instance, in works like *Flora* (fig.8) responded to McEvoy's infectious appeal and lightened his palette. The radiant young debutante contrasted with Lavery's *femme fatale* in *The Gold Turban,* but even here, accessories are removed in order to focus attention upon the made-up mask of the sitter.

With Lavery's passing, the generation which had brought the Royal Society of Portrait Painters into existence also passed. Lavery, Shannon, Sargent and the other portraitists of the 1890s had stood for a great tradition of figure painting described by Edward Knoblock in his epitaph on Lavery, a tradition in which "... an artist linked his art to the art before him and thus lead on with his own art to the art to come.

There was no striving to break with tradition and to be individual and different as there is with modern painters."[45] The central thrust of this consensus, which drew its authority from seventeenth century Spanish Caravaggesque portraiture, reworked by late nine-teenth century French realists and their followers and given a theoretical justification by Whistler, lay at the core of the Society's early exhibitions. It was not so simple or so cynical as Gissing's disreputable hero makes it appear. Public taste in portraiture, whilst admitting variations, had a single dominant direction. Its confidence was intimately bound up with the confidence of a secure and unshakably prosperous society – "an expanding orchid, at the root of which was a worm not yet hatched."[46]

NOTES

I am grateful to Pat Lambert of the Federation of British Artists for her assistance in gaining access to the records of the Royal Society of Portrait Painters. I would also like to thank present members of the Society, particularly David Poole, Edward Hall, George J. D. Bruce and Daphne Todd for their enthusiasm in the rediscovery of the Society's early history.

1. George Gissing, *Will Warburton*, 1905, pp.138-139

2. *The Magazine of Art*, 1891, Art Notes, p.xxv. The early history of the the Royal Society of Portrait Painters has essentially to be reconstructed from a series of Minute Books contained in the Federation of British Artists and from press coverage of the annual exhibitions. The Minute Books principally record the Society's dealings with gallery proprietors in connection with its annual exhibitions, the retrieval of subscriptions, the submission of accounts, the liaison with foreign exhibitors and the revision of the Society's rules. New members are simply noted for the record and the debate concerning their respective merits has not been minuted. The Society's history was summarized in a short article by Herbert A. Olivier R.I., in "The Royal Society of Portrait Painters", *The Studio*, vol. cxxx, September 1945, pp. 65-73.

3. Meeting held on 9 April 1891. The annual subscription of £5 entitled a member to six feet of line space, and £10 was set for more than six feet.

4. *The Magazine of Art*, 1891, Art Notes, p.xxxvii.

5. *The Athenaeum*, 18 July 1891, p.105.

6. *The Speaker*, 11 July 1891, p.49.

7. The lady artists, Louise Jopling, Anna Lea Merritt and others were accepted on the same terms as their male colleagues. Their contributions were noted by *The Magazine of Art*, 1891, Art Notes, p.xxxvii, and praised by Frederick Wedmore in *The Academy*, 4 July 1892, p.36.

8. Archibald John Stuart Wortley 1849-1905, son of the Rt. Hon. James Stuart Wortley, was John Everett Millais' only pupil. The families inter-married. In addition to his accomplishments as a painter, Wortley was regarded as one of the finest shots of his day. He wrote monographs for the "Fur and Feathers" series entitled *The Grouse*, *The Partridge* and *The Pheasant*.

9. For further reference to J.J. Shannon see Kenneth McConkey, *Edwardian Portraits*, 1987, pp.118-9, 150-1; Babara Dayar Gallati, "James Jebusa Shannon", *Antiques*, November 1988, pp.1133-1141.

10. *The Magazine of Art*, 1892, Art Notes, p.xxxviii.

11. For a discussion of this phenomenon see Kenneth McConkey, *op.cit.*, pp.22-38.

12. *The Speaker*, 2 July 1892, p.15.

13. Osbert Sitwell, ed., *A Free House!, being the Writings of Walter Richard Sickert*, 1947, pp.6-20.

14. ibid.

15. R.P. Minute Book

16. M. Phipps Jackson, "The Grafton Gallery", *The Magazine of Art*, 1892, p.350.

17. For further reference to these works see James Lomax and Richard Ormond, *John Singer Sargent and the Edwardian Age*, catalogue of an exhibition at Leeds, London and Detroit, 1979, pp. 55-56.

18. T. Martin Wood in *The Studio* Vol. LXIII, April 1908, p.226.

19. *Colour Magazine*, August 1916, p.40.

20. Osbert Sitwell ed., *op.cit.*, pp.78-82.

21. R.P. Minute Book, meetings of 5,6 and 15 October 1896.

22. *The Athenaeum*, 19 October 1895, p.539.

23. *The Athenaeum*, 21 November 1896, p.720.

24. *The Magazine of Art*, 1892, Art Notes, p.xxxviii.

25. Osbert Sitwell, ed., *op.cit.*, p.82.

26. *The Athenaeum*, 14 October 1903, p.657.

27. *The Athenaeum*, 22 November 1902, p.689.

28. *The Athenaeum*, 19 October 1895, p.539.

29. *The Art Journal*, 1891, pp.158, 199.

30. George Moore, *Modern Painting*, 1893, pp.190-191.

31. Frank Rinder, "J.J. Shannon A.R.A.", *The Art Journal*, 1901, p.41.

32. William Quiller Orchardson became President of the Society in 1905 after the death of Stuart Wortley.

33. R.P. Minute Book, 8 February 1911.

34. Herbert A. Olivier, *op.cit.*, p. 68.

35. "A Notable Portrait by Mr. William Orpen A.R.A.", *The Studio*, vol. LXII, 1914, p. 87.

36. T. Martin Wood, "The 'Fair Women' Exhibition of the International Society", *The Studio*, Vol. XLIII, April 1908, pp.225-232.

37. The formation of the Modern Society was announced in *The Art Journal*, 1907, p.28.

38. *The Art Journal*, 1907, p.88.

39. *The Athenaeum*, 21 October 1911, p.496, found that the Modern Society contained "the raw material of artistic ability", but it was "without a function to perform."

40. Herbert A. Olivier, *op.cit.*, p. 69.

41. *Colour Magazine*, November 1917, p.xvii.

42. *Colour Magazine*, February 1923, p.iii.

43. James Laver, *Portraits in Oil and Vinegar*, 1925, p.183.

44. Ulster Museum, Belfast, *Ambrose McEvoy*, catalogue of an exhibition introduced by Christine Campbell Thomson, 1968, n.p.

45. The Leicester Galleries, *Memorial Exhibition of the Paintings of the Late Sir John Lavery R.A.*, 1941, with an introduction by Edward Knoblock, p.9.

46. James Laver, *op.cit.*, 1925, p.6.

PAST MEMBERS

As the catalogue is printed prior to hanging the exhibition,
it is regretted that the picture numbering is not in strict order.

1

1
HON. JOHN COLLIER 1850-1934
Marion Collier
canvas, 24½ x 19¼ ins (61.9 x 49.2 cms)
Lent by The National Portrait Gallery, London

Collier trained at the Slade School, under Jean-Paul Laurens in Paris and in Munich. He achieved early success in history painting when *The Last Voyage of Henry Hudson* was purchased by the Chantrey Bequest. During the ensuing decades Collier gradually switched to portrait painting. He wrote a number of art primers including *The Art of Portrait Painting* (1905). He showed 165 pictures at R.P. exhibitions.

2

2

HON. JOHN COLLIER 1850-1934
Sir Joseph Hooker
oil on canvas, 24½ x 19¼ ins (73 x 69 cms)
Lent by Kind Permission of The President and Council of The
Royal Society, London

3

SIR JAMES JEBUSA SHANNON, RA 1862-1923
The Stairs
canvas, 71½ x 36 ins (181.8 x 91.4 cms)
Lent by Bradford Art Galleries and Museums

Shannon was born in Auburn, New York, of Irish parents.
He remained in London after his student years, 1878-1881,
at the Government Art Training School, South Kensington.
A founder member of the New English Art Club and the
Royal Society Portrait Painters, he became the Society's
third President in 1910. This followed closely upon his
election to the Royal Academy. His *The Flower Girl* was
purchased for the Chantrey Bequest in 1901. He showed 54
works at R.P. exhibitions

3

4

5

4

SOLOMON JOSEPH SOLOMON 1860-1927
Ramsay MacDonald
oil on canvas, 35½ x 28½ ins (90.2 x 72.4 cms)
Lent by The National Portrait Gallery

Solomon studied at the Royal Academy Schools and at the
Ecole des Beaux Arts in Paris. He was a founder member of
the New English Art Club who swiftly transferred to portraiture from allegorical subjects. He worked as a camouflage
artist in the Great War and became President of the Royal
Society of British Artists in 1919. He showed 27 works at
the R.P. exhibitions.

5

SIR LAWRENCE ALMA-TADEMA, OM, RA 1836-1912
A Family Group
oil on panel, 11½ x 11 ins (30.4 x 27.9 cms)
Lent by The Royal Academy of Arts, London.

Alma-Tadema trained at the Antwerp Academy of Fine Arts
under Baron Leys. He moved to London in 1870 and
quickly gained a reputation as a painter of classical genre
scenes. His *A Favourite Custom* was purchased by the
Chantrey Bequest for the Tate Gallery in 1909. He exhibited 11 works at R.P. exhibitions.

6

7

6

GEORGE FREDERICK WATTS, OM, RA, 1817-1904
Guiseppe Garibaldi
oil on canvas, 26½ x 39 ins (67 x 99 cms)
Lent by The Trustees of the Watts Gallery, Compton

Watts was apprenticed to the sculptor, William Behnes, before attending the Royal Academy Schools. He made his debut at the Royal Academy in 1837 and in 1843 he won first prize in the competition for the decoration of the Houses of Parliament. For the following four years he travelled extensively in Italy. Upon his return he painted *Time and Oblivion*, the first of the large allegorical pictures for which he was famed. By the time of his election to the R.A. in 1867 he was already respected for his portraits. He showed 40 works at R.P. exhibitions.

7

SIR JAMES GUTHRIE, PRSA, RA 1859-1930
The First Earl of Oxford and Asquith
oil on canvas, 19 x 14 ins (48.3 x 35.6 cms)
Lent by The National Portrait Gallery

Guthrie was essentially self taught, although he took lessons from the Victorian narrative painter, John Pettie. He was influenced by Bastien-Lepage in early canvases depicting rural life on the east coast of Scotland. He became a leading member of the Glasgow School and his later reputation was founded primarily upon portraiture. Guthrie was elected President of the Royal Scottish Academy in 1902, a post which he held until 1919. He showed 16 works at R.P. exhibitions.

8

8

PHIL MAY 1864-1903

Sir Frank Brangwyn

chalk drawing, 6½ x 5¼ ins (16.5 x 13.3 cms)
Lent by The National Portrait Gallery

Although he was primarily a black and white artist and
illustrator, May also painted portraits. He was a prominent
figure in the art world at the turn of the century, having his
portrait painted by J. J. Shannon. He worked mostly for
Punch.

9

SIR WILLIAM QUILLER ORCHARDSON, RA
1832-1910

Francis Paget

oil on canvas, 44 x 35 ins (111.7 x 90.2 cms)
Lent by The Governing Body of Christchurch, Oxford

Orchardson studied under Scott Lauder at the Trustees
Academy, Edinburgh. He moved to London in 1862, where
he established a reputation as a painter of historical
subjects. In the 1880s he produced a number of modern
life dramas on the *mariage de convenance* theme. By that
time he was also well known as a portraitist who acted as
the Society of Portrait Painters second President (1905-
1910) exhibiting 14 works at its exhibitions.

9

10

10
SIR WILLIAM ROTHENSTEIN 1872-1945
Eli the Thatcher
oil on canvas, 30¼ x 25 ins (76.5 x 63.3 cms)
Lent by Manchester City Art Galleries

Rothenstein studied briefly at the Slade School of Fine Art and at the atelier Julian in Paris. He was a painter of interiors, landscapes and portraits who was a close friend of Orpen and John. His *The Princess Badroulbadour,* 1908, was purchased by the Chantrey Bequest. Rothenstein was a war artist in both world wars and from 1920 was Principal of the Royal College of Art. He was particularly active in the revival of interest in mural painting in the inter-war period. He showed 50 works in R.P. exhibitions

11
HAROLD SPEED 1872-1957
Dr. David Little operating for cataract, 1919
oil on canvas, 53¼ x 48¼ ins (136.6 x 122.2 cms)
Lent by Manchester City Art Galleries

Speed studied at the National Art Training School, South Kensington and the Royal Academy Schools. He won a travelling scholarship to Italy and staged his first solo exhibition in 1907. His *The Alcantara, Toledo, by moonlight* was purchased by the Chantrey Bequest for the Tate Gallery in 1905. He became Master of the Art Workers' Guild in 1916 and was renowned for his portraits. He taught painting at Goldsmith's College. He showed 166 portraits at R.P. exhibitions.

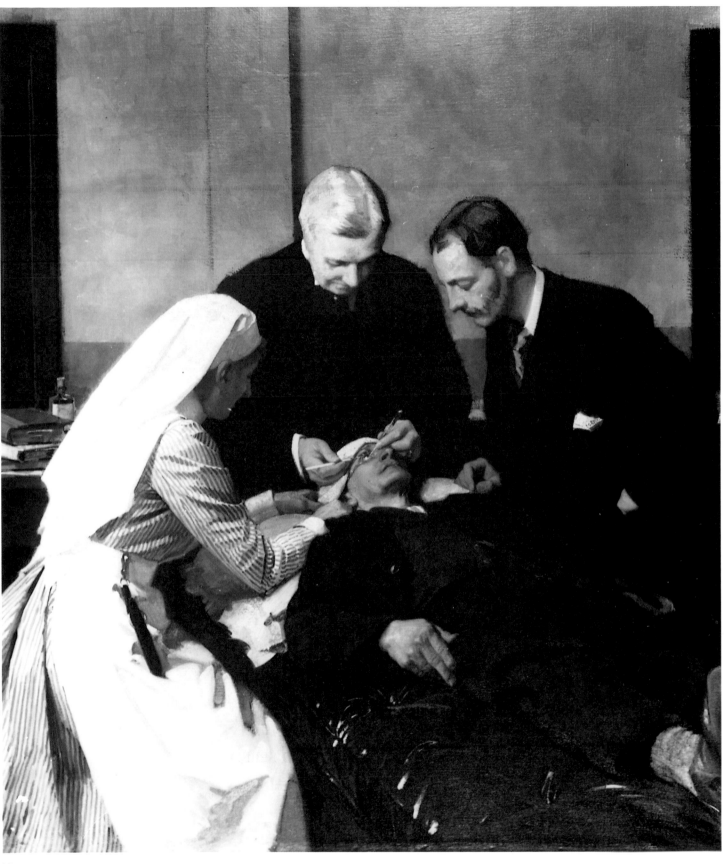

11

12

12
CHARLES WELLINGTON FURSE 1868-1904
Sir Francis Galtan
oil on canvas, 30 x 29¾ ins (76.2 x 75.3 cms)
Lent by The National Portrait Gallery

Furse studied at the Slade School of Fine Art under Legros
from 1884, at the atelier Julian, Paris and the Westminster
School of Art. He began to exhibit at the Royal Academy in
1888 and at the New English Art Club in 1891. His celebrated *Diana of the Uplands* was purchased by the
Chantrey Bequest for the Tate Gallery in 1903. The following year Furse died prematurely of tuberculosis. He showed
four pictures at the R.P.

13
CHARLES WELLINGTON FURSE 1868-1904
The Rt. Hon. Joseph Chamberlain, MP
oil on canvas, 106 x 71 ins (269 x 185 cms)
Lent by The Worshipful Company of Cordwainers, London

14

14
SIR ARTHUR STOCKDALE COPE, RA 1857-1940
Richard Pilkington Esq.
oil on canvas, 36 x 28 ins (91.7 x 71.1 cms)
Lent by Lady Pilkington

Cope was the son of the Victorian painter Charles West Cope. He studied at the Royal Academy Schools and from early in his career, specialized in portraiture and landscape painting. He ran his own art school in South Kensington and his pupils included Vanessa Bell and Nina Hamnett. His sitters included, King Edward VII and Lord Kitchener. He contributed 12 works to R.P. exhibitions.

15

15
HARRINGTON MANN 1867-1937
Lt.Col. Maitland
oil on canvas, 72¼ x 60 ins (183 x 152.5 cms)
Lent by The Trustees of the Imperial War Museum

Mann studied at Glasgow School of Art and the Slade School, London in the 1880s. During the following decade he worked in Glasgow among contemporary Glasgow School painters like Lavery and Walton. Like them, he eventually moved to London where he established a portrait practice, exhibiting at the International Society and latterly at the Royal Academy. He showed 87 works at R.P. exhibitions.

16 (not illustrated)
AUGUST NEVEN DU MONT 1868-1909
The Artist's Wife
oil on canvas, 23¼ x 16¼ ins (59 x 41 cms)
Lent by Mrs. C. Neven du Mont

Du Mont was born in Cologne and trained at the Dusseldorf Academy. His wife, Maria von Guilleaume, came from a wealthy family of Westphalian industrialists. He moved to London in April 1896 and was a close friend of John Lavery. He showed at the International Society and contributed 25 pictures to R.P. exhibitions.

17

17
SIR JOHN LAVERY, RA, RSA, RHA 1856-1941
The Gold Turban
oil on canvas, 30 x 25 ins (76 x 63.5 cms)
Private Collection, courtesy Pyms Gallery, London.

Lavery trained at the Haldane Academy, Glasgow and at the atelier Julian in Paris. His early work at Grez-sur-Loing was influenced by Bastien-Lepage, and in later years, he became a leading member of the Glasgow School. Like Guthrie, he worked primarily as a portraitist, becoming Vice-President of the International Society and President of the R.P. in 1931. He was an Official War Artist and during the inter war period, two of his pictures were purchased by the Chantrey Bequest for the Tate Gallery. Lavery showed 140 works at R.P. exhibitions.

18

18
SIR JOHN LAVERY, RA, RSA, RHA 1856-1941
The Royal Family at Buckingham Palace, 1913
oil on canvas, 37 x 41¾ ins (93.8 x 106.4 cms)
Lent by gracious permission of Her Majesty The Queen

19

19

JOHN SINGER SARGENT, RA 1856-1925
Arthur, Duke of Connaught
oil on canvas 62¾ x 43¾ ins (160 x 112 cms)
Reproduced by gracious permission of Her Majesty The Queen

Sargent studied in Rome and Florence and under Carolus Duran in Paris. He established a reputation as a portraitist in Paris prior to his removal to London in 1884. Sargent was influenced by his friend, Claude Monet to adopt an impressionist style. Impressionist effects were incorporated into his portraits in the 1890s and by 1900, he was regarded as the leading portrait painter of his day. His *Carnation Lily, Lily, Rose* had already been purchased by the Chantrey Bequest in 1887. Sargent also worked as a muralist for the City of Boston and as an Official War Artist in 1918. He showed 17 portraits at R.P. exhibitions.

21

20 (cover)
JOHN SINGER SARGENT, RA 1856-1925
Louise, Duchess of Connaught
oil on canvas 62¾ x 43¾ ins (160 x 112 cms)
Reproduced by gracious permission of Her Majesty The Queen

21
WILFRID GABRIEL DE GLEHN 1870-1951
Morning
oil on canvas, 30 x 36 ins (76 x 91.5 cms)
Lent by David Messum Fine Paintings Ltd.

De Glehn studied at the Government Art Training School, South Kensington and the Ecole des Beaux Arts, Paris. He was a pupil and close friend of Sargent, helping the latter to execute his Boston Public Library murals. De Glehn began to exhibit at the New English Art Club in 1900 with allegorical paintings in an Edwardian rococo style. He was also a fluent landscape and portrait painter. He showed 53 works at R.P. exhibitions.

23

22
SIR JOHN EVERETT MILLAIS, PRA 1829-1896
Bubbles
oil on canvas, 43 x 31 ins (109 x 79 cms)
Lent by A. & F. Pears Ltd.

Millais studied under Henry Sass and at the Royal Academy Schools. He was a leading member of the Pre-Raphaelite Brotherhood who, with *Christ at the House of his Parents* and *Ophelia,* produced some of the most controversial and ultimately popular Victorian pictures. In the 1860s Millais' style broadened under the influence of Reynolds and Velazquez and by the 1870s he had a formidable reputation as a portrait painter, going on to depict such notables as Gladstone, Disraeli and Tennyson. He showed 16 works at R.P. exhibitions.

23
SIR HUBERT VON HERKOMER, RA 1849-1914
Field Marshal H.R.H. The Duke of Cambridge, KG
oil on canvas, 100 x 62 ins (253 x 158 cms)
Lent by The Officers of the Corps of Royal Engineers.

Herkomer studied at the Government Art Training School, South Kensington, before becoming an illustrator for *The Graphic*. In the 1870s, he showed social realist pictures at the Royal Academy and gradually transferred to portraiture in the ensuing decade. He also founded and directed the Bushey School of Art and was Slade Professor of Fine Art at Oxford. Herkomer showed 23 works at R.P. exhibitions.

24

24
WILLIAM STRANG 1859-1921
Portrait of a Man
oil on canvas 30 x 25 ins (76 x 63.5 cms)
Lent by Andrew McIntosh Patrick

Strang studied at the Slade School of Fine Art, 1902-1906 and at the atelier Julien. He was widely known as an etcher who, to some extent, revived the archaisms of Legros. He travelled extensively in Europe, gaining material for his powerful representations of peasants. At the same time he achieved a reputation as a portraitist whose *Self-Portrait* of 1919 was purchased by the Chantrey Trustees for the Tate Gallery. He showed 15 works at R.P. exhibitions.

25
SIR OSWALD BIRLEY, RA 1880-1952
Her Majesty Queen Mary
oil on canvas 40¾ x 30 ins (103.5 x 76 cms)
Reproduced by gracious permission of Her Majesty the Queen

After taking a degree at Trinity College, Cambridge, Birley studied art in Dresden, Florence and at the atelier Julian in Paris. He quickly established a reputation as a portrait painter, adopting a style derived from that of John Singer Sargent. Birley contributed 101 works to R.P. exhibitions.

25

26

26
RICHARD JACK, RA 1866-1952
Lord Moynihan
oil on canvas, 49¼ x 39½ ins (125 x 100 cms)
Lent by The President and Council of The Royal College of
Surgeons of England

Jack studied at York College of Art, the Government Art
Training School, South Kensington and at the atelier Julian.
Initially he worked as an illustrator and as a miniaturist. His
Rehearsal with Nikisch was purchased by the Chantrey
Trustees in 1912. He became a Royal Academician in 1920
and by that stage was a regular exhibitor at the R.P., show-
ing 43 works at its exhibitions.

27
SIR WILLIAM ORPEN, RA, RHA 1878-1931
Bridgit - A Picture of Miss Elvery
oil on canvas 43¼ x 33¼ ins (110 x 84.5 cms)
Private collection, courtesy Pyms Gallery, London

Orpen trained at the Metropolitan School of Art, Dublin,
and the Slade School of Fine Art. He was a contemporary
of John and McEvoy who began exhibiting at the New
English Art Club in 1900. Orpen's tastes were eclectic and
early works like *The Mirror* reveal a range of Old Master
influences. Like John, Orpen was interested in developing
a mural style which he used for a sequence of works eulo-
gizing life in the West of Ireland. He was an Official War
Artist and in 1923 became the fourth President of the R.P.,
showing 51 pictures in its exhibitions.

28

29

28
SIR WILLIAM ORPEN, RA, RHA 1878-1931
The Refugee
oil on canvas 36 x 29¾ ins (91.5 x 76.5 cms)
Trustees of the Imperial War Museum

29
SIR WILLIAM NICHOLSON 1872-1949
Girl in a Straw Hat
pastel 24½ x 15 ins (62.2 x 38 cms)
Lent by Tom Coates Esq.

Nicholson studied under Sir Hubert von Herkomer before attending the atelier Julian in Paris. In the mid-nineties he and a fellow ex-student from Paris, James Pryde, worked as poster designers, being known as the Beggarstaff Brothers. Nicholson also achieved public acclaim for his woodcuts of famous personalities of the day. By 1900 he was turning more to painting and his portraits are distinguished by their Whistlerian sense of abstract relationships. He showed 19 works at R.P. exhibitions.

30

31

30
SIR WILLIAM NICHOLSON 1872-1949
The Viceroy's Orderly
oil on canvas 78 x 39 ins (198.1 x 99.1 cms)
Lent by Nottingham Castle Museum and Art Gallery

31
SIR WILLIAM NICHOLSON 1872-1949
Miss Wish Wynne
oil on canvas 23 x 21 ins (58.4 x 53.3 cms)
Lent by Nottingham Castle Museum and Art Gallery

32

33

32
PHILIP ALEXIUS DE LASZLO 1869-1937
Liza Minghetti
oil on canvas 46 x 36 ins (117 x 91.5 cms)
Lent by The Philip Trust

De Laszlo trained at the National Academy of Arts, Budapest and at the atelier Julian, Paris. He worked in Munich and Dresden before coming to London to execute commissions around the turn of the century. He finally settled in London in 1907 painting portraits of the British aristocracy and international figures such as Theodore Roosevelt. His portrait of *Benito Mussolini* won for him the Grand Cross of the Crown of Italy. He showed 14 works at the R.P.

33
SIR FRANK OWEN SALISBURY, RA 1874-1963
Sir William Blake Richmond
oil on canvas 59¼ x 49¾ ins (152 x 126 cms)
Lent by the Art Workers Guild, London

Salisbury trained at the Royal Academy Schools from 1892. During his student years he visited Italy and studied the work of the Old Masters. He made his debut at the Royal Academy in 1899. His talents as a muralist were quickly recognized and he supplied decorations for the House of Lords, the Royal Exchange and the Guildhall. He depicted members of the Royal Family on many occasions, as well as statesmen like Churchill, Woodrow Wilson and Eisenhower. He contributed 76 works to R.P. exhibitions.

51

34

34
SIR EDWARD JOHN POYNTER, PRA 1836-1919
Edward Henry Pember
oil on canvas 50 x 47½ ins (127 x 121.6 cms)
Lent by The Society of Dilettante

Poynter was trained at the Royal Academy Schools and at Gleyre's atelier in Paris. He rose to prominence in the Royal Academy in the 1860s with historical pictures such as *Isreal in Egypt* and *The Catapult*. He was the first Slade Professor of Fine Art at University College, London and Principal of the National Art Training School, South Kensington 1876-1891. For nine years from 1896 he was both President of the Royal Academy and Director of the National Gallery. During this time he was increasingly involved in portraiture and exhibited twice at R.P. exhibitions.

35 (not illustrated)
REGINALD GRENVILLE EVES, RA 1876-1941
Lord Darling
oil on canvas 49 x 39 ins (124.5 x 99 cms)
Lent by The Arts Club, London

Eves was a portrait and landscape painter. He studied at the Slade School of Fine Art from 1891 and saw the change of regime from Legros to Brown, Tonks and Steer in 1892. Sargent was his principal influence after leaving the Slade in 1895. He showed regularly at the Royal Academy from 1901 and became an Academician in 1939, two years after the purchase of his portrait of *Max Beerbohm* for the Tate Gallery under the terms of the Chantrey Bequest. He showed 128 works at the R.P.

36

37

36
FLORA LION 1876-1958
Sir Henry Wood
Lithograph 13½ x 10¼ ins (34.3 x 26 cms)
Lent by the National Portrait Gallery

37
FLORA LION 1876-1958
Liza Lehman
Lithograph 14 x 10 ins (35.6 x 25.4 cms)
Lent by the National Portrait Gallery

Flora Lion studied at the Royal Academy Schools and the atelier Julian in Paris. She was a popular portrait painter in the years prior to the Great War. She also exhibited landscapes and figure subjects. Eighty-three works by her were exhibited at R.P. exhibitions.

38 (not illustrated)
ARTHUR TREVITHIN NOWELL 1862-1940
Private View Day at the Royal Academy
oil on canvas 76¼ x 50¾ ins (193.6 x 128.8 cms)
Lent by The Arts Club, London

Nowell painted landscape and genre pictures as well as portraits. He studied at Manchester School of Art, the Royal Academy Schools and in Paris. He exhibited regularly at the Royal Academy and at the Royal Institute of Painters in Watercolours. Twenty-two works by him were shown at R.P. exhibitions.

39

40

39

GERALD LESLIE BROCKHURST, RA 1890-1978

Clytie

oil on panel 20 x 15½ ins (50.7 x 39.6 cms)

Lent by Manchester City Art Galleries

Brockhurst studied at Birmingham School of Art and at the Royal Academy Schools, winning a series of prestigious prizes. His renown as a portraitist was supported by his great accomplishment as an etcher. In works such as *Dorette*, 1933, he revived a High Renaissance style. He portrayed famous sitters such as the Duchess of Windsor and Marlene Dietrich. In 1939 he moved to New York. He showed 23 pictures at R.P. exhibitions.

40

DOUGLAS STANNUS GRAY 1890-1959

Miss Kathleen Chambers

oil on canvas 45 x 34¾ ins (114 x 88 cms)

Private Collection

Gray studied at Croydon School of Art and the Royal Academy Schools. He returned to painting after military service in the Great War and made his debut at the Royal Academy in 1920. His portrait *Rosalind* was purchased by the Chantrey Trustees for the Tate Gallery in 1929. Gray was a belated follower of Sargent's *alla prima* manner in portrait and landscape painting. He taught briefly at Brighton Art College in 1947. He became a member of the R.P. in 1933 and exhibited 9 pictures in its exhibitions.

41

41

THOMAS CANTRELL DUGDALE, RA 1880-1952

Portrait Group

oil on canvas 31½ x 43 ins (80 x 109 cms)

Private Collection

Dugdale studied at Manchester School of Art, the Royal College of Art and at the ateliers of Julian and Colarossi in Paris. After the Great War his paintings of Palestine were exhibited at the Leicester Galleries. He was married to fellow R.P. exhibitor, Amy K. Browning. He exhibited regularly at the Royal Academy and showed 78 works in R.P. exhibitions.

42

HAROLD KNIGHT, RA 1874-1961

Ethel Bartlett, Pianist

oil on canvas 78 x 46 ins (198.1 x 116.8 cms)

Lent by Nottingham Castle Museum and Art Gallery

Knight studied at Nottingham School of Art and at the atelier Julian, Paris. While at Nottingham he met his future wife, Laura. A landscape, portrait and genre painter, he made his Royal Academy debut in 1896. He worked initially at Staithes, on the Yorkshire coast, before transferring to Newlyn in 1908. *In the Spring*, painted shortly after his arrival, shows the influence of Impressionism. Thereafter he painted interiors and *A Student* was purchased for the Tate Gallery under the terms of the Chantrey Bequest in 1938. He showed 11 works at R.P. exhibitions.

42

43

44

43
ETHEL WALKER, DBE 1867-1951
The Artist's Stepmother
oil on canvas 40 x 30 ins (101.6 x 76 cms)
Lent by Mr and Mrs Peyton Skipwith

Ethel Walker studied at Westminster School of Art and at the Slade School of Fine Art. She also was a pupil of Sickert and Wyndham Lewis. In 1900, she was elected to the New English Art Club and in the late twenties, she joined the 7 and 5 Society and the London Group. Her portrait of *Jean Warner Laurie* was purchased for the Tate Gallery in 1931. She contributed 25 works to R.P. exhibitions.

44
MAURICE FREDERICK CODNER 1888-1958
Sir Albert Richardson
oil on canvas 50½ x 40¼ ins (128 x 102 cms)
Lent by The Art Workers' Guild, London

Codner was primarily known as a portraitist. He became a member of the R.P. in 1937 and showed 24 works at its annual exhibitions.

46

45

AMBROSE McEVOY, ARA 1878-1927
Mademoiselle Pourtales
oil on canvas 60¾ x 40½ ins (154 x 103 cms)
Lent by Bradford Art Galleries and Museums

In his youth, Ambrose McEvoy was encouraged to take up painting by Whistler. He entered the Slade School of Fine Art in 1893 and became a regular New English Art Club exhibitor. He was a friend of Orpen, John and Rothenstein. He also worked with Sickert for a time at Dieppe. In later years he was renowned for his high-key female portraits. He showed 11 portraits at R.P. exhibitions.

46

SIR ALFRED J. MUNNINGS, RA 1878-1959
Arrival at Epsom Downs for Derby Week
oil on canvas 40¾ x 51½ ins (103.5 x 130.8 cms)
Lent by Birmingham City Museums and Art Gallery

Munnings was a landscapist and painter of rural life as well as a portrait painter. He trained at Norwich School of Art and at the Atelier Julian in Paris. His initial reputation was as a recorder of East Anglian life. He served as a War Artist for the Canadian government and as his *Epsom Downs - City and Suburban Day* was being purchased for the Tate Gallery under the terms of the Chantrey Bequest in 1920, he was switching his interests to equestrian portraits. He showed six pictures at R.P. exhibitions.

47

48

47
COWAN DOBSON 1893-1980
Chiffon
canvas 24 x 20 ins (61 x 50.7 cms)
Lent by Mrs Cowan Dobson

Cowan Dobson was the son of the Scots genre painter
Henry John Dobson (1858-1928). Primarily a portrait painter
he worked in London, Edinburgh and Glasgow and is
included in the collections of the Scottish National Portrait
Gallery, The Royal Glasgow Institute and The Imperial War
Museum. He showed 15 works at R.P. exhibitions.

48
AUGUSTUS EDWIN JOHN, OM, RA 1878-1961
David at a Table
oil on canvas 25 x 11¾ ins (63.5 x 30 cms)
Lent by Lord and Lady Irvine of Lairg

Augustus John was trained at the Slade School of Fine Art
under Brown, Tonks and Steer, 1894-1898. He made his
debut at the New English Art Club in 1899 and was
Professor of Painting at Liverpool University 1901-1904.
Widely regarded as one of the leading painters of his day,
his work was favoured by the Chantrey Trustees who
purchased portraits of Lord David Cecil, W.B. Yeats,
Edward Grove and Theodore Powys for the Tate Gallery.
Often these works succeed in the sheer bravura of their
technique. John was also renowned as an allegorical
painter of murals. He showed 14 works at R.P. exhibitions.

49

49
AUGUSTUS EDWIN JOHN, OM, RA 1878-1961
Sara in a red dress
oil on canvas 24 x 20 ins (61 x 51 cms)
Private Collection

50
GLYN WARRAN PHILPOT, RA 1884-1937
Gabrielle and Rosemary
oil on canvas 56¼ x 44 ins (143 x 112 cms)
Lent by The Visitors of the Ashmolean Museum, Oxford

Philpot was trained at Lambeth School of Art and under Jean-Paul Laurens in Paris. He travelled extensively in Spain and Italy. He showed at the Royal Academy from 1904 and at the International Society and the Modern Society of Portrait Painters. He was selected by the Fine Art Commissioners to execute one of the murals at St. Stephen's Hall in the Palace of Westminster in 1927. In the early 1930s his style changed rapidly, under the influence of *école de Paris* modernism. He showed 11 works at R.P. exhibitions.

50

51

52

51

SIR GEORGE CLAUSEN, RA 1852-1944

Lady in a Black Dress

oil on canvas 25 x 12 ins (63.5 x 30.5 cms)

Private Collection, Courtesy of The Fine Art Society, London

Clausen studied at the Government Art Training School, South Kensington and at the atelier Julian, Paris. He was primarily a painter of rustic subjects. His *The Girl at the Gate,* reflecting the influence of Bastien-Lepage, was one of the first of a series of purchases under the terms of the Chantrey Bequest. Clausen was one of the most important Professors of Painting at the Royal Academy and his *Lectures* were widely read by art students. He was an Official War Artist and contributed a mural to St. Stephen's Hall, Westminster, in 1927. He showed eight pictures at R.P. exhibitions.

52

SIR GERALD FESTUS KELLY, RA 1879-1972

Ralph Vaughan Williams

oil on canvas 36 x 44 ins (91.5 x 111.8 cms)

Lent by The Royal College of Music.

Kelly studied at Trinity Hall, Cambridge and in Paris where he moved in radical art circles. He was a founder member of the Modern Society of Portrait Painters and his portrait of W. Somerset Maugham, entitled *The Jester,* of 1911 was later purchased by the Chantrey Bequest for the Tate Gallery. Kelly acquired an international reputation, painting portraits in the United States and in the Far East. He became President of the Royal Academy in 1949. He contributed 18 works to R.P. exhibitions.

53

53

SIMON ELWES, RA 1902-1975

Sergeant Edwards, MM

oil on panel 20½ x 17½ ins (52 x 44.5 cms)

Lent by The Trustees of the Imperial War Museum

Elwes studied at the Slade School of Fine Art 1918-21 and continued his artistic education in Paris until 1926. The following year he made his debut at the Royal Academy. He was an Official War Artist in India and East Asia during the Second World War. He showed 30 works at R.P. exhibitions.

54

ANTHONY DEVAS 1911-1958

Camilla Sykes and Mark

oil on canvas 34 x 20 ins (86.5 x 51 cms)

Lent by Bradford Art Galleries and Museums

Anthony Devas studied at the Slade School of Fine Art 1927-1930. He was primarily a figure, portrait and flower painter, whose early work reflects the influence of the late style of Henry Tonks. His portrait of *Mrs. Wilson* was purchased for the Tate Gallery under the terms of the Chantrey Bequest in 1939. In the year before his death he portrayed Her Majesty the Queen for the Honorable Artillery Company.

54

55

55
SIR HERBERT JAMES GUNN, RA 1893-1964
General Sir William Dobbie, GCMG, KCB, DSO, LLD
oil on canvas 38½ x 30¾ ins (98 x 78 cms)
Lent by The Officers of the Corps of Royal Engineers

Gunn studied at Glasgow School of Art, Edinburgh College of Art and at the atelier Julian under Jean-Paul Laurens. A landscape and portrait painter, his early work executed in France, reveals a fine sense of abstract arrangement and colour balance. In later years Gunn was acclaimed for his portraits and in 1953 he painted the state portrait of Her Majesty the Queen.

56

56
SIR HERBERT JAMES GUNN, RA 1893-1964
Her Majesty the Queen
oil on canvas 30 x 25 ins (76 x 63.5 cms)
Lent by The Fine Art Society, London

57

57
WILLIAM DRING, RA 1904-1990
Dr. Cyril Garbett
oil on canvas 35½ x 26½ ins (90 x 67 cms)
Lent by The Lord Bishop of Winchester and the Church
Commissioners

Dring studied at the Slade School of Fine Art in the 1920s.
As a draughtsman his preferred medium was pastel. He
worked as an Official War Artist in the Second World War.
He taught painting at Southampton School of Art and in the
post-war period exhibited portraits and landscapes at the
Royal Academy.

58
ALFRED KINGSLEY LAWRENCE, RA 1893-?
John V. Sheffield
oil on canvas 50¾ x 40 ins (129.5 x 101.5 cms)
Lent by J. Julian L.G. Sheffield Esq.

Lawrence studied at the Royal College of Art and was a
Prix de Rome winner in 1923. He exhibited regularly at the
Royal Academy throughout the thirties and was elected
Academician in 1938. He shared Rothenstein's desire to
promote mural painting and much of his time during the
inter-war period was spent upon mural commissions.

58

59

59
DAVID JAGGER *exhibited* 1917-1940
Jewish Refugee, Vienna
oil on canvas 24 x 20 ins (61 x 50.8 cms)
Lent by Nottingham Castle Museum and Art Gallery

Jagger was a London-based figure, portrait and landscape
painter. He exhibited at the Royal Academy and the Royal
Society of British Artists as well as showing 15 portraits at
R.P. exhibitions.

60
DAVID JAGGER *exhibited* 1917-1940
The Black Mantilla
oil on canvas 30 x 25½ ins (76 x 63.5 cms)
Private Collection

61

61
AMY KATHERINE BROWNING 1882-1970
Alone
oil on canvas 36 x 28 ins (91.4 x 71 cms)
Lent by The Royal Academy of Arts, London

Browning was primarily known as a portrait and flower painter. She studied at the Royal College of Art and in Paris, winning a Silver Medal at the Paris Salon of 1912. She was married to the painter T. C. Dugdale. She showed 6 works at R.P. exhibitions.

62
PIETRO ANNIGONI 1910-1988
Juanita Forbes
oil on panel 26¾ x 19 ins (68 x 48 cms)
Lent by Mrs. Richard Stickney

Previously exhibited at Wildenstein in 1954.

62

63

63
PAUL WYETH 1920-1982
The Artist's Daughters
oil on canvas 20 x 16 ins (51 x 41 cms)
Lent by Mrs P Wyeth

He trained initially at Hammersmith School of Building and
Arts and Crafts, as it was then known. After war service he
completed his training at the Royal College of Art.
Though primarily a portrait painter he carried out numer-
ous mural commissions. These took him to Australia and
the USA. In the United Kingdom examples are to be found
in York Assembly Rooms and at Eridge Castle in Kent.
He was a member of the Salon des Beaux Arts and in 1987,
as a member of the RBA, gained the de Laszlo Award.

64
MAURICE LITTEN 1919-1980
Brenda
oil on canvas 36 x 28¼ ins (91.5 x 71.5 cms)
Lent by Mrs Alma Litten
Previously exhibited at the Royal Society of Portrait Painters.

He trained at Goldsmiths' School of Art and, after war
service in India, where he gained an All India Award for
Portraiture, he resumed his studies at St. Martin's School of
Art.
His professional career was devoted almost entirely to
portraiture.

64

65

65
EDWARD IRVINE HALLIDAY, CBE, PPRP 1902-1984
Leon Goosens
oil on canvas 36 x 25 ins (91.5 x 63.5 cms)
Lent by Mrs Corrina A. Lopez (née Goosens)

Halliday studied at Liverpool City School of Art, Colarossi's atelier in Paris, the Royal College of Art and the British School in Rome. In addition to portraiture, Halliday developed a reputation as a painter of decorative schemes.

66

66
PATRICK PHILLIPS 1906-1976
Self Portrait Study
pencil on paper 14½ x 9½ ins (37 x 24 cms)
Lent by Mr John Phillips

Trained at Byam Shaw School of Drawing and Painting under F E Jackson, Charles Shannon and Glyn Philpot. Joined teaching staff 1933, becoming principal from 1946-1955. His portrait of *Mrs Carter Giffard* was purchased by the Chantrey Bequest in 1977. He excelled as a draughtsman and teacher. Hon Treasurer 1972-1976.

67

68

67
JESSE DALE CAST 1900-1976
Miss Beatrice Dale Cast
oil on canvas 22 x 16 ins (56 x 40.8 cms)
Lent by The Trustees of the Tate Gallery

Cast studied at St.Martin's, Camberwell and the Slade School of Fine Art. After leaving the Slade in 1926 he lived in Belgium and Majorca. Throughout the thirties he exhibited at the Royal Academy and the R.P. After War service in aircraft production, he took up teaching, becoming head of fine art at Hornsey College of Art.

68
ALLAN GWYNNE-JONES, DSO, ARA 1892-1982
Fred Lindsay, Headmaster, The Preparatory School, Sherborne
oil on canvas 24¾ x 31 ins (63 x 79 cms)
Lent by R.T.M. Lindsay Esq.

After qualifying as a solicitor, Gwynne-Jones began to paint in watercolour. He was wounded twice in the Great War and was awarded the DSO. He attended the Slade School of Fine Art, 1919-1922 and joined the staff of the Royal College of Art in 1923, becoming its Professor of Painting. He transferred to the Slade staff in 1930, where he remained until 1958. He is known for landscape and still-life painting as well as penetrating portraits.

69

70

69
LAURA KNIGHT, DBE, RA 1877-1970
Take Off
oil on canvas 72 x 60 ins (183 x 152.5 cms)
Lent by The Trustees of the Imperial War Museum

Laura Johnson trained at Nottingham School of Art and in 1903 was married to her fellow student, Harold Knight. She is primarily known as a genre painter, specializing in coastal scenes at Staithes and Newlyn, and scenes from the lives of circus performers. Two typical works, *Spring* and *The Gypsy*, were purchased for the Tate Gallery by the Chantrey Trustees. Knight became an Official War Artist in the Second World War and was famed for her depictions of the Nuremburg trials.

70
LAURA KNIGHT, DBE, RA 1877-1970
The Gypsy
oil on canvas 24 x 16 ins (61 x 40.6 cms)
Lent by The Trustees of the Tate Gallery

71

72

71
WILLIAM C. EVANS ?-1979
Lord Blackett
oil on canvas 49¼ x 39½ ins (125 x 100 cms)
Lent by kind permission of the President and Council of
The Royal Society

72
JOHN KENNETH GREEN ?-1985
Benjamin Britten with Sir Peter Pears
oil on canvas 28¼ ins x 38¼ ins (71.5 x 96.9 cms)
Lent by The National Portrait Gallery

Green is known as a portrait and landscape painter who also specialised in woodcuts. He showed 10 works at R.P. exhibitions.

73

74

73
DORIS CLARE ZINKEISEN 1898-1991
Mrs Harold Taylor
oil on canvas 48 x 34 ins (122 x 86.3 cms)
Private Collection

Zinkeisen and her younger sister Anna (1901-1976) both studied at the Royal Academy Schools. She exhibited regularly at the Royal Academy and at the Paris Salon and was well known for stage designs as well as portraiture. She showed 8 works at R.P. exhibitions.

74
HERBERT ANDREW FREETH, RA 1912-1986
The Rt. Hon. Enoch Powell, MBE, MP
oil on canvas 30 x 22 ins (76.2 x 55.9 cms)
Lent by Mrs R. Freeth

Freeth studied at Birmingham College of Art and at the British School in Rome. He made his debut at the Royal Academy in 1936 and is known primarily as a portrait painter and engraver. In 1943 he went to the Middle East as an Official War Artist with the R.A.F. After his return he exhibited regularly at the Academy, the Royal Watercolour Society and the Royal Society of British Artists.

PRESENT MEMBERS

75

75
NORMAN HEPPLE, RA, PPRP *born* 1908
Margaret
oil on canvas 52 x 42 ins (132.1 x 107 cms)
Lent by the artist
Previously exhibited at the RP

Studied at Goldsmiths School of Art, Royal Academy
Schools, taught by Harold Speed RP and Sir Walter Russel RA.

76

77

76
PETER GREENHAM, CBE, RA *born* 1909
Mrs Dorothy Hall
oil on canvas 21 x 16 ins (53.5 x 40 .3cms)
Lent by the artist
Exhibited at the RA Summer Exhibition 1960 and Arts Council
Exhibition 1985

Studied at Byam Shaw School of Drawing and Painting
under F. Ernest Jackson.

77
JOHN WARD, CBE, RA *born* 1917
The East Kent Group
oil on canvas 40 x 50 ins (101.6 x 127 cms)
Lent by the artist

Studied at Hereford School of Art and Royal College of Art.

78

78

CLAUDE HARRISON, HON. RP *born* 1922
The Family of David Mansel Pleydell, 1972
oil on canvas 30 x 43 ins (76.2 x 109.2cms)
Previously exhibited at the RA 1974

79

DEREK CLARKE, RSW, ARSA *born* 1912
Jennie, Andrew and Catriona
oil on canvas 36 x 28ins (91.4 x 71.1cms)
Lent by Ann and Archie MacKenzie
Previously exhibited at the Royal Society of Portrait Painters 1952
Royal Society of Arts 1953

Studied at the Slade School of Art 1931 to 1935.

79

80

80
EDWARD HALL, (Vice President), *born* 1922
Kathy and Nicky playing chess
oil on canvas 40 x 50 ins (102 x 127 cms)
Owned by the artist
Previously exhibited at the RA 1961

Studied at Wimbledon School of Art: Slade School of Fine Art.

Former Honorary Treasurer and Honorary Secretary.
Vice President 1990.

81
GEORGE J. D. BRUCE *born* 1930
Arthur Michael Ramsey DD, Lord Archbishop of Canterbury 1961-1974
oil on canvas 58½ x 43 ins (148.5 x 109 cms)
Lent by the Church Commissioners and the Archbishop of Canterbury
Previously exhibited at the Royal Academy Summer Exhibition 1983

Studied at Byam Shaw School of Drawing and Painting under Brian Thomas, Patrick Phillips and Peter Greenham.

Honorary Secretary 1970-1984.
Vice President 1985-1990.

81

82

83

82
JEHAN DALY
John Ward
oil on canvas 12 x 10 ins (30.5 x 2.5 cms)
Lent by John Ward

Studied at Kidderminster School of Art: Royal College of Art.

83
RICARDO MACARRON
Vaoleta Muñoc Gordobil
oil on canvas 51 x 38 ins (130 x 97 cms)

Studied at School of Fine Art San Fernando, Madrid.

84

84
DAVID DONALDSON, RSA, RGI, LLD, D.LITT
born 1916
Caroline with Ciao
oil on canvas 50 x 50 ins (127 x 127cms)
Property of Caroline Donaldson
Previously exhibited Royal Glasgow Institute 1968, Royal
Scottish Academy 1969

85
MICHAEL NOAKES, PPROI *born* 1933
Her Royal Highness The Princess Royal.
Colonel-in-Chief, The Royal Signals.
Painted, as Princess Anne, in 1979
oil on canvas 72 x 36 ins (183 x 91.4cms)
Lent by the Headquarters Mess, The Royal Signals.
Previously exhibited at the Royal Society of Portrait Painters 1980

85

86

86
EDWIN GREENMAN *born* 1909
The Artists Mother in her 95th year
oil on canvas 40 x 35 ins (101.5 x 89 cms)
Owned by the artist
Previously exhibited at the Royal Academy 1963

Studied at Beckenham School of Art 1926-1929 under Henry Carr, RA; Royal College of Art 1929-1934 under Sir John Rothenstein and Percy Horton.
Head of Sir John Cass College School of Art 1950-1969.

Former Honorary Secretary and Honorary Treasurer of the RP.

87

87

DAVID POOLE, (President), *born* 1931

H.R.H. Prince Philip The Duke of Edinburgh

(left) pastel (centre and right) oil on canvas
overall 17 x 39 ins (43 x 99 cms)
Lent by gracious permission of Her Majesty The Queen

Studied Wimbledon School of Art, Royal College of Art.

88 (frontispiece)

DAVID POOLE, (President), *born* 1931

*Her Majesty the Queen, Captain General Royal
Regiment of Artillery 1975*

oil on canvas 50 x 40ins (127 x 102cms)
Lent by the officers of the Royal Regiment of Artillery
Previously exhibited National Portrait Gallery 1986

89

89

WILLIAM BOWYER, RA, RWS, NEAC *born 1926*
Robert Tear as Samson, Carol Vaness as Delilah
from the opera by Handel
oil on canvas 28 x 28 ins (71 x 71cms)
Owned by the artist
Previously exhibited at the Royal Academy 1990

Studied at Burslem School of Art, Royal College of Art.
Hon. Secretary New English Art Club, member of the Royal
Society of Painters in Watercolour
1973 Associate of the Royal Academy
1981 Elected member of the Royal Academy

90

90
ALEXANDER GOUDIE *born* 1933
Marie Seynec
oil on canvas 53 x 83 ins (134.5 x 211 cms)
Owned by the artist

Studied at Glasgow School of Art.

91 (not illustrated)
ALEX KOOLMAN, RBA
Paul at Reigate
oil on canvas 20 x 24 ins (51 x 61 cms)

Studied at Wimbledon School of Art, Allan Frazer College
of Art Scotland.

92

92
JUNE MENDOZA, AO, ROI, HON.D.LITT.BATH
Miss Ainslie Gotto
oil on canvas 45 x 60 ins (114.3 x 152.4 cms)
Lent by Miss Ainslie Gotto
Previously exhibited at the RP

Studied at St Martins School of Art.

93

93
DAVID GRAHAM
Martha Luz
oil on canvas 28 x 36 ins (71 x 91cms)
Lent by the Artist

Studied at the Royal College of Art.

94

95

94
FREDERICK DEANE *born* 1924
Self Portrait
oil on canvas 25 x 19 ins (63.5 x 48.2 cms)
Lent by the artist

Studied at the College of Art, Manchester, Royal Academy
Schools.

95
RUPERT SHEPHARD *born* 1909
Ann Cornwell, Samantha, Kate and Barnaby
oil on canvas 28 x 36 ins (71 x 91.5 cms)
Lent by the artist
Previously exhibited at the RP 1981

Studied at Slade School of Art.

96

97

96
LEONARD BODEN, FRSA
Martin A. Buckmaster ARCA, HON.RIBA
oil on canvas 40 x 30 ins (102 x 76 cms)
Lent by the Arts Club, London
Previously exhibited at the RP 1955

Studied at Glasgow School of Art and Heatherley's under
Sir William Hutchison, John Revel and Frederick Whiting.

97
DOUGLAS ANDERSON *born* 1934
The Masters Denis, Walcot Hall, Lincolnshire
oil on canvas 59 x 49½ ins (150 x 126cms)
Lent by Mr Darby Denis
Previously exhibited at the RP 1967

Trained by Annigoni in Florence.

98

99

98
CARLOS SANCHA, (Hon Treasurer), *born* 1920
Mrs Andrew Baylis
oil on canvas 51 x 40 ins (129.5 x 102 cms)
Lent by Mr Andrew Baylis

Studied at Byam Shaw School of Drawing and Painting.

99
RICHARD FOSTER *born* 1945
Lord Sackville
oil on canvas 30 x 40 ins (76 x 101.5 cms)
Lent by Lord Sackville
Previously exhibited at Spinks 1991

Studied at Studio Simi, Florence and City and Guilds, London.

100

101

100
TREVOR WILLOUGHBY *born* 1926
Terance Weil of the Melos Ensemble
oil on canvas 36 x 28 ins (91.4 x 71 cms)
Lent by the artist
Previously exhibited at the RP 1963

Studied at Hull Regional College of Art and London School
of Printing.

101
JOHN EDWARDS, CERT.RA SCHOOLS *born* 1940
Sir Denis Trustcott, GBE, TD. Sir Noel Bowater Bt,
GBE, MC and Sir Lionel Denny,CBE, MC. Former
Lord Mayors of London and former Masters of the
Vintners' company in the Vintners' Hall
oil on canvas 28 x 36 ins (71 x 91.5 cms)
Lent by the Vintners Company
Previously exhibited at the RP 1980

Studied under Pietro Annigoni and RA Schools.

102

102
JOHN WALTON, DFA (Lond.) *born* 1925
Victoria
oil on canvas 13½ x 11½ ins (34.3 x 29.2 cms)
Lent by the artist
Previously exhibited at the RA and Paris Salon

Studied at Ruskin School of Painting and Slade School of Art.

103
ALBERTO MORROCCO, RSA, RSW, RGI, LLD, D.UNIV
born 1917
Vera
oil on canvas 54 x 34 ins (137.2 x 86.3 cms)
Lent by the artist
Previously exhibited at the RSA 1971 and RP

Studied at Gray's School of Art, Aberdeen under James Cowie, Robert Sivell and D. M. Sutherland.

103

104

105

104
ANTHONY MORRIS, NDD, RAS *born* 1938
Reverend Kenneth N J Loveless, MBE, VRD, BA,
FSA Scot., Hon.RNR
oil on canvas 40 x 30 ins (101.6 x 76.2 cms)
Lent by the artist

Studied at Oxford College of Art, Royal Academy Schools
under Peter Greenham, CBE, RA.

105
TREVOR STUBLEY, DA (Edin.) ARBA, RSW *born* 1932
Jane, Mrs Robert Hassell McCosh
watercolour and pencil 15 x 11 ins (38 x 28cms)
Lent by the artist
Previously exhibited at the RP 1983

Studied at Leeds College of Art (1949-51) and Edinburgh
College of Art (1951-955).

106

106
MICHAEL REYNOLDS, RBA *born* 1933
The Misses Crystal
oil on board 48 x 72 ins (122 x 183cms)
Lent by Mr and Mrs Crystal

Studied at Brighton College of Art, Rome Scholarship 1962-64.

107
DAPHNE TODD, NEAC, (Hon Secretary)
S and O Mathews: A Close Couple
oil on panel 49 x 42ins (125 x 107 cms)
Previously exhibited at Mall Galleries

Studied at Slade School of Art.

107

108

109

108

WALTER WOODINGTON, RBA *born* 1916

Charles Hill Esq.

oil on canvas 36 x 28 ins (91.4 x 71 cms)
Previously exhibited RA Summer exhibition 1983

Studied at City and Guilds of London Art School.

109

PETER JOHN GARRARD, PPRBA, RWA, NEAC

born 1929

Dr Graham Miller, DM, FRCP

oil on canvas
Lent by Dr and Mrs Graham Miller
Previously exhibited at the RP 1987

Studied at Byam Shaw School of Drawing and Painting.

110

110
HOWARD MORGAN *born* 1949
A. N. C. Embiricos
oil on canvas 53 x 77 ins (134.7 x 95.7cms)
Lent by A. N. C. Embiricos

Studied at Newcastle upon Tyne.

111
JOHN G. BOYD, RGI *born* 1940
Jonathan with Bagpipes
oil on canvas 40 x 30 ins (101.5 x 76 cms)
Lent by the artist
Previously exhibited at the Corners Gallery, Glasgow 1985 and
RP 1986

Studied at Gray's School of Art, Aberdeen.

111

112

112
JOHN SERGEANT *born* 1937
Alfred Sergeant
Pastel 15 x 12 ins (38 x 30.5 cms)
Lent by the artist
Previously exhibited at the RP 1981

Studied at RA Schools.

113
TOM COATES, PRBA, RWS, NEAC *born* 1941
Mary Jackson, Painter
oil on canvas 84 x 48 ins (213 x 122 cms)
Lent by the artist

Studied at Birmingham College of Art and the Royal Academy Schools.

113

114

114
HANS SCHWARZ *born* 1922
Sandra and the girls
oil on board 36 x 48 ins (91.5 x 122 cms)
Lent by Sandra and Bob Scales

Studied in Vienna and Birmingham.

115
MARTIN YEOMAN
Arthur John Yeoman
oil on canvas 25 x 21 (63 x 53 cms)
Lent by the artist
Previously exhibited National Portrait Gallery 1981

Studied at Royal Academy Schools, taught by Peter Greenham.

Portrait of Arthur John Yeoman
Martin Yeoman 1980

115

ANDERSON, Douglas, c/o Royal Society of Portrait Painters, 17, Carlton House Terrace, London SW1Y 5BD

BODEN, Leonard, 36 Arden Road, London N3 3AN

BOWYER, William, RA, RWS, NEAC, 12 Cleveland Avenue, Chiswick, London W4

BOYD, John G., Hayston, 26 Cleveden Road, Glasgow, G12 0PX

BRUCE, George J.D., 6 Pembroke Walk, London W8 6PQ

CLARKE, Derek, RSW, 90 Raeburn Place, Edinburgh, EH4 1HH

COATES, Thomas J., PRBA, ROI, RWS, NEAC, Bladon Studio, Hurstbourne Tarrant, Nr. Andover, Hants, SP11 0AH

DALY, Jehan, Woodlands Manor, Adisham, Near Canterbury, Kent

DEANE, Frederick, Penrallt Goch, Llan Ffestiniog, Gwynedd

DONALDSON, David, RSA, LL.D, 7 Chelsea Manor Studios, Flood Street, SW3 *and* 5 Clevedon Drive, Glasgow, G12 0SB

EDWARDS, John C. Chesterville, Gallery and Studio, 163 Chester Road North, Kidderminster, Worcestershire, DY10 1TP

FOSTER, Richard, 5 Thurloe Square, London SW7 2TA

GARRARD, Peter, PPRBA, RWA, NEAC, 340 Westbourne Park Road, London W11 1EQ

GOUDIE, Alexander, Arnewood House, 4 Cleveland Road, Glasgow, G12 0NT

GRAHAM, David, RBA, 2 Curran Studios, Lucan Place, Chelsea, London, SW3

GREENHAM, Peter, CBE, RA, PPRBA, c/o The Royal Academy of Arts, Burlington House, Piccadilly, London W1

GREENMAN, Edwin, 7 Southfields Close, Donnington, Chichester, West Sussex, PO19 2SD

HALL, Edward, *(Vice-President)*, 51 St. George's Drive, London SW1V 4DE

HEPPLE, Norman, RA, PPRP, 10 Sheen Common Drive, Richmond, Surrey TW10 5BN

KOOLMAN, Alex, RBA, 20 Elmwood Road, Chiswick, London W4 3DZ

MACARRON, Ricardo, Agustin de Bethencourt No.5, Madrid 3, Spain

MENDOZA, June, ROI, 34 Inner Park Road, London SW19 6DD

MORGAN, Howard James, 12 Rectory Grove, London, SW4

MORRIS, Anthony, Drostre House, Talyllyn, Brecon, Powys LD3 7SY

MORROCCO, Alberto, RSA, RSW, Binrock, 456 Perth Road, Dundee DD2 1NG

NOAKES, Michael, PPROI, 146 Hamilton Terrace, St. John's Wood, London NW8 9UX

POOLE, David *(President)*, The Granary, Oxton Barns, Kenton, Exeter, Devon EX6 8EX
  and Studio 6, Burlington Lodge, Rigault Road, Fulham, London SW6 4JJ

REYNOLDS, Michael, 17 Carlton House Terrace, London SW1Y 5BD

SANCHA, Carlos, *(Hon. Treasurer)*, 8 Melbury Road, Kensington, London W14 8LR

SCHWARZ Hans, RBA, RWS, NEAC, 1 King George Street, Greenwich, London SE10 8QJ

SERGEANT, John, Gilfach Farm, Birlth, Rhulen, Builth Wells, Powys LD2 3UU

SHEPHARD, Rupert, NEAC, 68 Limerston Street, London SW10 0HJ

STUBLEY, Trevor, ARBA, 85 Arlington Avenue, Islington, London N1
  and The Trevor Stubley Gallery, Greenfield Road, Holmfirth, Huddersfield HD7 2XQ

TODD, J. Daphne, NEAC, *(Hon. Secretary)*, Salters Green Farm, Mayfield, East Sussex TN20 6NP

WALTON, John, 30 Park Road, Radlett, Hertfordshire

WARD, John, CBE, RA, RWS, Bilting Court, Nr. Ashford, Kent, TN25 4HF

WILLOUGHBY, Trevor, 4 Offerton Road, Clapham Old Town, London SW4 0DH

WOODINGTON, Walter, RBA, 5 Kenver Avenue, Finchley, London N12 0PG

YEOMAN, Martin, RBA, NEAC, c/o The Federation of British Artists, 17 Carlton House Terrace, London SW1Y 5BD

Secretary
Patricia Lambert
17 Carlton House Terrace, London SW1Y 5BD
Telephone: 071-930 6844

Past Presidents and Vice-Presidents

A. Stuart Wortley
Sir W. Q. Orchardson, RA, HRSA
Sir James J. Shannon, RA
Sir Wm. Orpen, RA, RHA, etc.
Hon. John Collier, OBE
Sir John Lavery, RA, RSA, RHA, etc.
George Harcourt, RA
Sir Oswald Birley, RA
Augustus John, OM, RA
T. C. Dugdale, RA
Simon Elwes, RA, LL.D
Sir James Gunn, RA, LL.D
Sir William O. Hutchinson, PPRSA, HON. RA, LL.D
Edward Halliday, CBE, PPRBA
Norman Hepple, RA
John Ward, CBE, RA, RWS
George J. D. Bruce

Deceased Honorary Members

Sir Lawrence Alma-Tadema, OM, RA
Sir George Clausen, RA
Sir Arthur Cope, RA
Cowan Dobson, RBA
William Dring, RA, RWS
Hugh de T. Glazebrook
Kenneth Green
Sir James Guthrie, PRSA, RA
Allan Gwynne-Jones, DSO, RA
J. McLure Hamilton
Augustus John, OM, RA
Dame Laura Knight, RA
Leonard C. Lindsay, FSA
Sir Wm. Llewellyn, PRA
Sir John Everett Millais, PRA
A.T. Nowell
Herbert A. Oliver, RI
Sir Edward Poynter, PRA
Hugh G. Riviere
C. Sanders, RA
John S. Sargent, RA
Howard Somerville
A.R. Thomson, RA
G.F. Watts, OM, RA
T. Fiddes Watt, RSA
J. McNeill Whistler, HRSA, LL.D

Honorary Members
Claude Harrison

INDEX

(Year of election)   *illustrated page*

* Honorary Members

GENERAL INFORMATION

One of the aims of The Royal Society of Portrait Painters is the promotion of fine arts and in particular the fine art of portrait painting and drawing.

Fees for portraits are available at the Secretary's office, or at any other time photographs of work are available and enquiries may be made by personal visit or by letter to:

Annabel Elton
Royal Society of Portrait Painters
17 Carlton House Terrace, London SW1Y 5BD
or telephone 071-930 6844 (3 lines)

Communications will be regarded as confidential.

VALUE ADDED TAX
A number of painters' fees are subject to VAT. These will be indicated by the Secretary when quoting artists' individual fees for portraiture.

EDITORIAL PANEL
David Poole, PRP
George J. D. Bruce
Edward Hall, VPRP
Daphne J. Todd, (Hon. Secretary)

CENTENARY EXHIBITION
The present Exhibition will remain open from 4th May - 31st May 1991, including Saturdays and Sundays, and bank holidays from 10am to 7pm.

cover: *Louise, Duchess of Connaught* (detail) by John Singer Sargent
Reproduced by gracious permission of Her Majesty The Queen

Catalogue designed by Tim Harvey
Printed by The White Dove Press

ISBN 0 901415 04 9